js.
o\
D

PICTURE A COUNTRY

Japan

Henry Pluckrose

W
FRANKLIN WATTS
LONDON·SYDNEY

This is the Japanese flag.

First Published in 1998
by Franklin Watts
This edition 2001

Franklin Watts
96 Leonard Street
London EC2A 4XD

Franklin Watts Australia
56 O'Riordan Street
Alexandria, Sydney
NSW 2015

© Franklin Watts 1998

ISBN 0 7496 4282 3

A CIP catalogue record for this book is
available from the British Library

Dewey Decimal Classification Number: 915.2

10 9 8 7 6 5 4 3

Series Editor: Rachel Cooke
Designer: Kirstie Billingham
Picture research: Juliet Duff

Printed in Dubai

Photographic acknowledgements:

Cover: Top Getty Images (Chad Ehlers), middle Zefa
Pictures (Orion Press), bottom Getty Images.

AA Photo Library pp. 15, 21;
Colorific pp. 10 and 19 (Jean Paul Nacivet);
Eye Ubiquitous p. 23 (Frank Leather);
Getty Images pp. 8, 14 (Chad Ehlers), 22 (Charles Gupton),
24 (Chris Cole), 26;
Images Colour Library pp. 12 -13, 29;
Japan Information and Cultural Centre p. 17;
Magnum Photos p. 16 (Marc Riboud);
Spectrum Colour Library p. 28 (J. Raga);
Telegraph Colour Library pp. 11 (Japack Photo Library),
27 (VCL);
Zefa Pictures pp. 20, 25 (Orion Press).

All other photography by Steve Shott.

Map by Julian Baker.

Contents

Where is Japan?

This is a map of Japan.
Japan is in Asia.
Japan is made up of four main islands,
and many smaller ones.

Here are some Japanese
stamps and money.
Japanese money is
called yen.

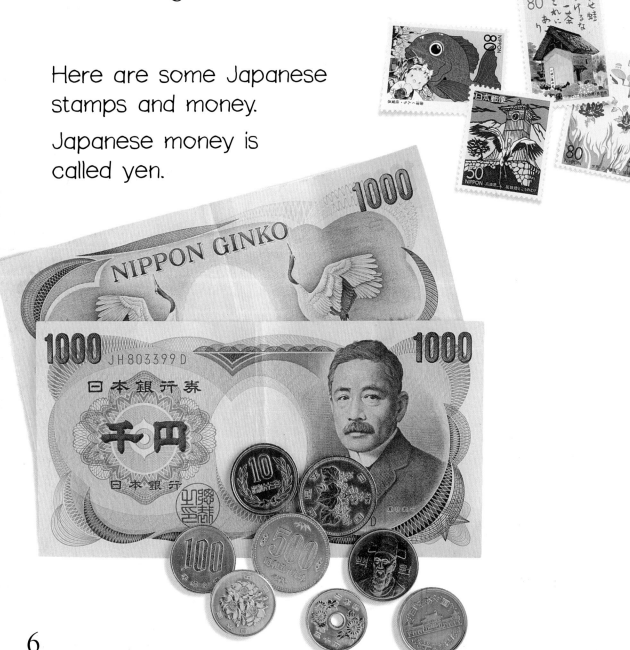

CHINA

RUSSIA

HOKKAIDO

SEA OF JAPAN

HONSHU

JAPAN

■Tokyo

Mount Fuji ▲   •Kamakura

Kyoto ●
Osaka ●

Hiroshima ●

SHIKOKU

●Fukuoka

KYUSHU

PACIFIC OCEAN

This is Mount Fuji. It is Japan's highest mountain. It is 3776 metres high. It is also a volcano.

The Japanese landscape

Japan is a country of mountains and lakes. On the northern islands the winters are cold and icy. On the southern islands the weather is warm throughout the year.

The Japanese people

People have lived in Japan
for thousands of years. Today,
over 124 million people live in Japan.

More people work in
factories and offices than
as fishermen and farmers.

These Japanese women work all day collecting seaweed
on the beaches of Hokkaido. Seaweed is good to eat.

Where they live

Many Japanese people live in cities -
Tokyo, Hiroshima, Fukuoka.
This is Osaka, the largest sea port
in Japan.

Most people live in flats.
There is not enough land for
every family to live in a house.

The capital city

Tokyo is the capital of Japan.
It is one of the world's
largest cities.
Over 12 million people live there.
It is a very busy city.

Yanaka is the old part of Tokyo. It has no
tower blocks and houses are made of wood.

Japanese factories

Japanese factories make many of the things we use every day - television sets, computers, videos, cameras and cars.

This factory produces video cameras.

Rice farming

The Japanese eat rice
with most of their meals.
Rice is grown by Japanese farmers
on the island of Honshu.
The rice is planted in fields
which are flooded with water.

This is a picture of a special rice planting festival.
The workers are wearing traditional costume.

At home

These Japanese children
are playing cards at home.

When you enter a Japanese home,
you take off your shoes.
You leave them by the front door.
You can wear slippers inside the house.

Japanese food

A Japanese meal is made up
of a lot of different kinds of food.
There will be rice, noodles or soya beans,
a soup, raw fish, rolls of seaweed and rice,
meat cooked in batter and fresh fruit.

Food is eaten with chopsticks.
This is a Japanese packed lunch!

Out and about

Japanese people like going
to the Kabuki theatre.
They also enjoy watching
Sumo wrestling.

To win a match, a Sumo wrestler
pushes his opponent out of the ring.

Kabuki plays tell stories of Japan long ago.

Japanese temples, such as Kingaku Temple in Kyoto, are often surrounded by water and beautiful gardens.

Japanese temples

Japan is a land of many temples.
These temples were built
to remind people of the
teachings of Buddha.
Some temples also remind them
of the beauty of nature.

This huge statue
of Buddha
is at Kamakura.

Visiting Japan

If you visit Japan,
you might ride
on a "bullet train".
A bullet train is very fast.
You might also see one of
Japan's colourful festivals.

This is the Gion Festival in Kyoto.

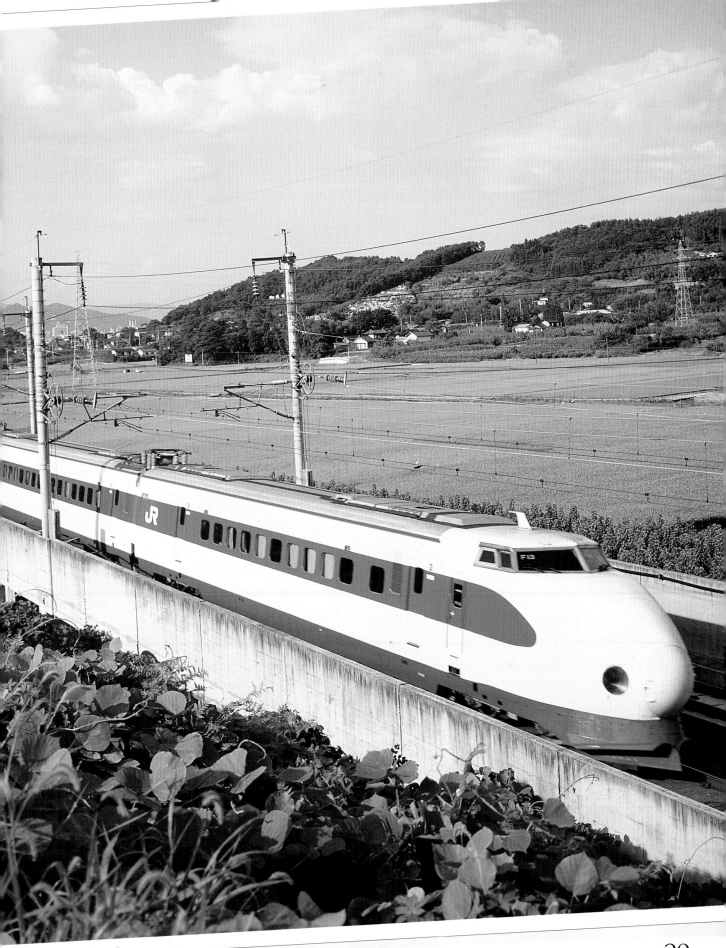

Index

About this book

The last decade of the 20th century has been marked by an explosion in communications technology. The effect of this revolution upon the young child should not be underestimated. The television set brings a cascade of ever-changing images from around the world into the home, but the information presented is only on the screen for a few moments before the programme moves on to consider some other issue.

Instant pictures, instant information do not easily satisfy young children's emotional and intellectual needs. Young children take time to assimilate knowledge, to relate what they already know to ideas and information which are new.

The books in this series seek to provide snapshots of everyday life in countries in different parts of the world. The images have been selected to encourage the young reader to look, to question, to talk. Unlike the TV picture, each page can be studied for as long as is necessary and subsequently returned to as a point of reference. For example, a Japanese street might be compared with the one in their own local area; a discussion might develop about the ways in which food is prepared and eaten in a country whose culture and customs are different from their own.

The comparison of similarity and difference is the recurring theme in each of the titles in this series. People in different lands are superficially different. Where they live (the climate and terrain) obviously shapes the sort of houses that are built, but people across the world need shelter; coins may look different, but in each country people use money.

At a time when the world seems to be shrinking, it is important for children to be given the opportunity to focus upon those things which are common to all the peoples of the world. By exploring the themes touched upon in the book, children will begin to appreciate that there are strands in the everyday life of human beings which are universal.